Assessment Book

Editorial Offices: Glenview, Illinois • Parsippany, New Jersey • New York, New York
Sales Offices: Parsippany, New Jersey • Duluth, Georgia • Glenview, Illinois •
Coppell, Texas • Ontario, California • Mesa, Arizona

www.sfsocialstudies.com

Program Authors

Dr. Candy Dawson Boyd
Professor, School of Education
Director of Reading Programs
St. Mary's College
Moraga, California

Dr. Geneva Gay
Professor of Education
University of Washington
Seattle, Washington

Rita Geiger
Director of Social Studies and
Foreign Languages
Norman Public Schools
Norman, Oklahoma

Dr. James B. Kracht
Associate Dean for
Undergraduate Programs
and Teacher Education
College of Education
Texas A&M University
College Station, Texas

Dr. Valerie Ooka Pang
Professor of Teacher Education
San Diego State University
San Diego, California

Dr. C. Frederick Risinger
Director, Professional
Development and Social
Studies Education
Indiana University
Bloomington, Indiana

Sara Miranda Sanchez
Elementary and Early
Childhood Curriculum
Coordinator
Albuquerque Public Schools
Albuquerque, New Mexico

Contributing Authors

Dr. Carol Berkin
Professor of History
Baruch College and the
Graduate Center
The City University of New York
New York, New York

Lee A. Chase
Staff Development Specialist
Chesterfield County
Public Schools
Chesterfield County, Virginia

Dr. Jim Cummins
Professor of Curriculum
Ontario Institute for Studies
in Education
University of Toronto
Toronto, Canada

Dr. Allen D. Glenn
Professor and Dean Emeritus
Curriculum and Instruction
College of Education
University of Washington
Seattle, Washington

Dr. Carole L. Hahn
Professor, Educational Studies
Emory University
Atlanta, Georgia

Dr. M. Gail Hickey
Professor of Education
Indiana University-Purdue
University
Fort Wayne, Indiana

Dr. Bonnie Meszaros
Associate Director
Center for Economic Education
and Entrepreneurship
University of Delaware
Newark, Delaware

ISBN 0-328-08193-0

12 13 14 15 16   V0YM   15 14 13 12 11

© Scott Foresman 2

Contents

To the Teacher

One way to evaluate the success of your social studies instruction lies in using the assessment options provided in **Scott Foresman** *Social Studies*. These options will help you measure students' progress toward social studies instructional goals.

The assessment tools provided with **Scott Foresman** *Social Studies* can

- help you determine which students need more help and where classroom instruction needs to be reinforced, reviewed, or expanded.
- help you evaluate how well students comprehend, communicate, and apply what they have learned.

Scott Foresman *Social Studies* provides a comprehensive assessment package as shown below.

Assessment Options Available in Scott Foresman *Social Studies*

Formal Assessments	✓ What did you learn? PE/TE ✓ Unit Review, PE/TE ✓ Unit Tests, Assessment Book ✓ Test Talk Practice Book
Informal Assessments	✓ Teacher's Edition Questions ✓ Close and Assess, TE ✓ Try it! PE/TE ✓ Think and Share, PE/TE ✓ Courage in Action, PE/TE ✓ Hands-on History, PE/TE
Portfolio Assessments	✓ Portfolio Assessment, TE ✓ Leveled Practice, TE ✓ Workbook Pages ✓ Unit Review, PE/TE ✓ Curriculum Connection, TE
Performance Assessments	✓ Hands-on Unit Project, PE/TE ✓ Internet Activity, PE ✓ Unit Review: Think and Share, PE/TE ✓ Scoring Guides, TE

Overview of Assessment Book

Unit Tests

The Unit Tests are a tool to evaluate students' understanding of social studies concepts and their ability to apply and analyze the concepts. There is a four-page, reproducible test for each unit in the Student Book.

Students are asked to fill in blanks, complete sentences, choose a correct answer from a series of possible responses, draw an answer, match items, and read/complete a map, chart, or graph.

Some of the questions carry the same Test Prep symbol as found in the Student Book. The icon tells students that a particular question is formatted the same way it would appear on a standardized test.

At the back of the Assessment Book, there is an answer key for each Unit Test.

Part 1: Content Test
The two-page content test includes a series of multiple choice questions covering levels of thinking from knowledge to comprehension, application, and analysis.

Part 2: Skills Test
The two-page skills test checks students' knowledge of and ability to apply the social studies skills taught in the Student Book.

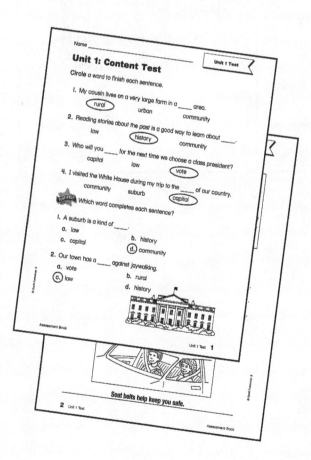

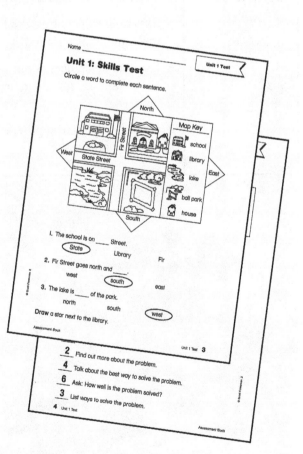

Unit Tests: Objectives Assessed

	Content Objectives	**Skills Objectives**
Unit 1 Test	• Determine the meanings of words. • Recognize diversity in communities. • Compare rural, urban, and suburban communities. • Identify rules and their purpose. • Identify state and national symbols.	• Use symbols, find locations, and determine directions on maps. • Locate communities, states, and countries on maps. Demonstrate map skills. • Use context clues to develop meanings of new words.
Unit 2 Test	• Determine the meanings of words. • Learn how people depend on the physical environment and its resources to meet their needs. • Identify ways to conserve and replenish natural resources.	• Identify cause-and-effect relationships. • Interpret and construct bar graphs. • Identify landforms and bodies of water on a map.
Unit 3 Test	• Determine the meanings of words. • Explain how countries are linked by trade and transportation. • Explain the choices people can make about earning, spending, and saving money. • Identify people who provide services to our community.	• Interpret print material by predicting. • Use a decision-making process. • Use a map to follow a route.

	Skills Objectives	**Content Objectives**
Unit 4 Test	• Determine the meanings of words. • Identify the functions of government. • Identify selected symbols such as state and national birds and flowers and patriotic symbols such as the U.S. flag and Uncle Sam. • Describe how governments establish order, provide security, and manage conflict.	• Use tables to categorize information. • Interpret print material by identifying the main idea and details. • Find locations on maps.
Unit 5 Test	• Determine the meanings of words. • Compare Native American cultures from different regions and times. • Identify historic figures who have exemplified good citizenship. • Explain the significance of national celebrations.	• Create and interpret a time line. • Sequence information. • Use a map scale to determine distance.
Unit 6 Test	• Determine the meanings of words. • Identify and explain the significance of various community, state, and national landmarks. • Explain how selected customs and celebrations reflect an American love of individualism, inventiveness, and freedom. • Describe and measure calendar time.	• Obtain information about a topic from print sources. • Summarize by recalling and retelling information in a logical sequence. • Obtain information about a topic using a diagram. • Describe and measure calendar time.

NOTES

Unit 1: Content Test

Circle a word to finish each sentence.

1. My cousin lives on a very large farm in a _____ area.

     rural   urban   community

2. Reading stories about the past is a good way to learn about _____.

     law   history   community

3. Who will you _____ for the next time we choose a class president?

     capital   law   vote

4. I visited the White House during my trip to the _____ of our country.

     community   suburb   capital

 Which word completes each sentence?

1. A suburb is a kind of _____.

     a. law   **b.** history

     c. capital   **d.** community

2. Our town has a _____ against jaywalking.

     a. vote   **b.** rural

     c. law   **d.** history

Name _____

Color the picture that shows a rural community.

Write a word to finish each sentence.

The name of my state is _____.

My state bird is _____.

My state flower is _____.

Write why it is important to follow this rule.

Unit 1: Skills Test

Circle a word to complete each sentence.

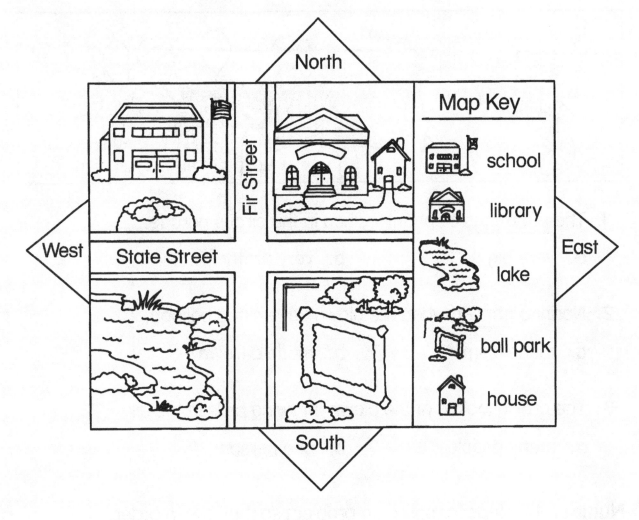

1. The school is on _____ Street.

    State   Library   Fir

2. Fir Street goes north and _____.

    west   south   east

3. The lake is _____ of the park.

    north   south   west

Draw a star next to the library.

© Scott Foresman 2

Look at each underlined word.

Circle the words that tell what it means.

1. The enormous elephant walked in the circus parade.

   a. very big   b. very pretty

2. Norihito grinned when the clown gave him a balloon.

   a. made a smile   b. made a frown

3. The crowd looked at the clown throwing balls in the air.

   a. many people   b. one person

Number the steps for solving a problem so they are in order.

_____ Name the problem.

_____ Solve the problem.

_____ Find out more about the problem.

_____ Talk about the best way to solve the problem.

_____ Ask: How well is the problem solved?

_____ List ways to solve the problem.

Unit 2: Content Test

Draw a line under the word that belongs in the sentence.

1. The protection of land, trees, and water is _____ .

       conservation

       landform

       geography

2. A family member who lived long ago is my _____ .

       natural resource

       geography

       ancestor

3. Wheat is one _____ that a farmer may grow.

       crop

       landform

       consumer

 Which word completes each sentence?

1. Air is a very important _____ .

   a. geography   **b.** natural resource

   c. crop   **d.** landform

2. A peninsula is a kind of _____ .

   a. producer   **b.** landform

   c. conservation   **d.** consumer

Think about how natural resources are used.

Write *soil*, *forests*, or *water* under the picture.

_____   _____   _____

Look at the picture.

Write two ways to show conservation.

_____

_____

Unit 2: Skills Test

Circle the cause in each sentence.

Draw a line under the effect.

I was hungry so I ate my sandwich.

It started to snow so I put on my boots.

The bird flew away because the cat jumped up.

Use the bar graph to answer the questions.

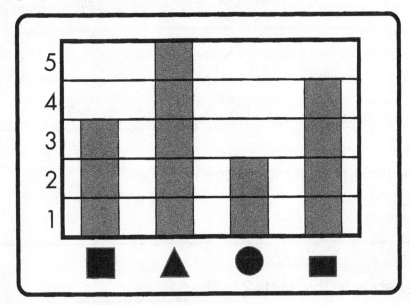

1. How many rectangles are there? _____

2. How many triangles are there? _____

3. Are there more squares or rectangles? _____

4. Are there fewer circles or squares? _____

Write answers to the questions about the map.

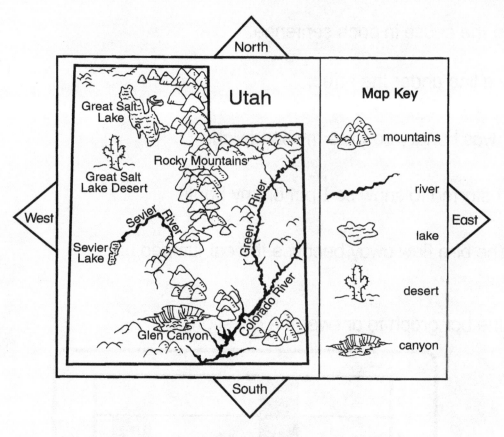

1. What state does the map show? _____

2. What are two lakes in this state?

   _____

3. What desert is in this state? _____

4. What are three rivers in this state?

   _____

5. A canyon is a deep valley. What canyon is in this state?

   _____

Unit 3: Content Test

Write the word that goes with each definition.

trade	services	income	factory

1. the money that someone earns _____

2. a building where people produce goods _____

3. jobs that people do to help others _____

4. to buy, sell, or exchange goods _____

 Which word completes each sentence?

1. Trains and trucks are a means of _____.

    a. services
    c. goods
    b. taxes
    d. transportation

2. In some places, there is a sales _____ on goods you buy.

    a. tax
    c. trade
    b. factory
    d. barter

Name _____

Check the things that link countries.

_____ airplane   _____ goods   _____ ship

_____ truck   _____ factory   _____ train

Write each word in the correct column.

| shoes | rug | food | car | pet | home |

Needs   **Wants**

_____   _____

_____   _____

_____   _____

Write the names of three service workers.

_____

_____

Circle two things people can do with their income.

buy goods   save it   use it to barter

© Scott Foresman 2

Unit 3: Skills Test

Write to predict what Mario will do.

> Mario is having a party in his backyard. The
> party will start in two hours. Suddenly, the wind
> starts to blow. Then some thick, black clouds roll in.

_____

_____

Explain your prediction.

_____

_____

Look at these steps for making a decision.

Number the steps in the correct order.

_____ Make a decision.

_____ List your choices.

_____ Gather information.

_____ Tell what decision you need to make.

_____ Tell what might happen with each choice.

Name _____

Use the map to complete the sentences.

Write *north*, *south*, *east*, or *west*.

1. The bike store is _____ of the gym.

2. The zoo is _____ of Tania's house.

3. The fruit stand is _____ of the gym.

4. Oak Lane is _____ of Park Street.

Unit 4: Content Test

Circle the word to finish each sentence.

1. The leader of the United States is the ____.

   mayor   President

2. A ____ honors a person or event.

   monument   motto

3. Someone living in a community is a ____.

   Congress   citizen

4. The right to make choices is called ____.

   freedom   motto

 Which word completes each sentence?

1. Your state is run by the state ____.

   a. citizen   **b.** monument

   c. mayor   **d.** government

2. The person who leads your state is the ____.

   a. governor   **b.** motto

   c. President   **d.** mayor

Draw lines to match.

President •   • writes and votes on laws.

Congress •   • leads the country.

Supreme Court •   • says if laws are fair.

Circle the symbols of the United States.

Write T if the sentence is true.

Write F if the sentence is false.

_____ The government settles disagreements.

_____ Our government makes laws.

_____ The U.S. government has two parts.

_____ Governments help us stay safe.

_____ The Congress is our highest court.

Unit 4: Skills Test

Read the sentences below.

Draw small pictures to fill in the table.

Our Favorite Things

Classmate	Favorite Food	Favorite Sport	Favorite Animal
Barb	(apple)		(bird)
Benny		(football)	
Me			

Benny likes to eat hamburgers. I like to eat _____.

Barb likes basketball. I like to play _____.

Benny and Barb like the same animal. The animal I like is _____.

Read about a sunset.

Underline the main idea, and circle the details.

It was a perfect sunset. The sky was pink and red.

A cool wind started to blow. Light, puffy clouds danced

against the setting sun.

Use the map to tell where things are.

Where can people find _____?

I. benches _____

2. a lake _____

3. a path _____

4. flowers _____

© Scott Foresman 2

Unit 5: Content Test

Circle a word to finish each sentence.

1. Squanto helped the _____ of Plymouth.

   colonists   resources

2. Many colonists wanted their _____ from England.

   shelter   independence

3. William Clark was a famous _____.

   explorer   colony

4. A place where people live is a _____.

   factory   shelter

5. The _____ moved west in covered wagons.

   railroads   pioneers

 Which word completes each sentence?

1. Eating turkey on Thanksgiving is a _____.

   a. tradition   **b.** shelter

   c. colonist   **d.** pioneer

2. St. Augustine was a Spanish _____.

   a. shelter   **b.** tradition

   c. explorer   **d.** colony

Write X by each sentence that is true about Native Americans.

_____ Native Americans used natural resources to build shelters.

_____ The Sioux wore clothing made from buffalo skins.

_____ Corn, beans, and squash were grown by the Pueblo.

_____ All Native American groups lived on the plains.

_____ The Powhatan lived along the Atlantic Coast.

Draw lines to match.

Squanto   helped the Jamestown colonists.

Harriet Tubman   helped the Pilgrims survive.

John Smith   helped Lewis and Clark explore.

Sacagawea   led escaping slaves to freedom.

Answer the questions.

What do we celebrate on Independence Day?

_____

Why do Americans celebrate Thanksgiving?

_____

Unit 5: Skills Test

Answer the questions about the time line.

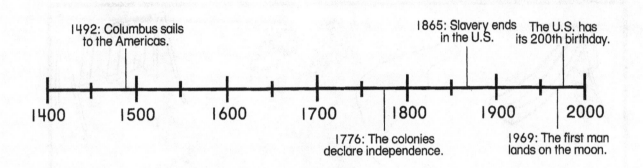

1. What happened in 1865?

_____

2. When did the first man land on the moon?

_____

3. What is the first event shown on the time line?

_____

4. What does this time line show?

_____

Write what comes *first*, *next*, and *last*.

_____ I rinse my mouth.

_____ I brush my teeth.

_____ I put toothpaste on my toothbrush.

Use a Map Scale

Look at the map and the map scale.

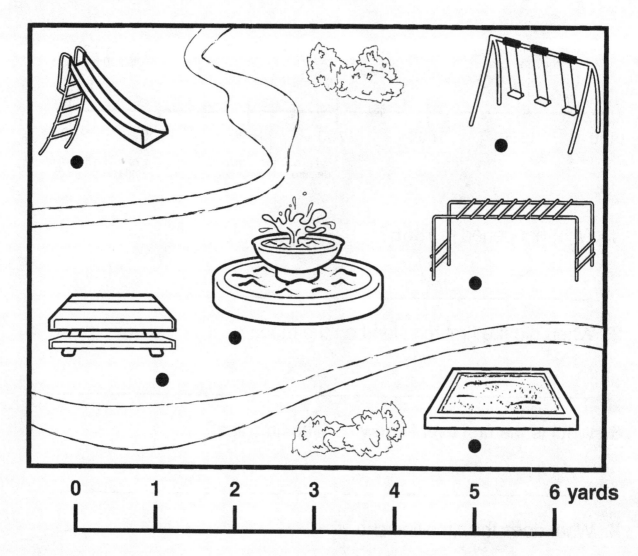

Write the answers.

1. What part of the map helps show distance? _____

2. How far are the swings from the water fountain? _____

3. How far is the slide from the sandbox? _____

4. How far is the picnic bench from the water fountain? _____

Unit 6: Content Test

Write the word that goes with each definition.

landmark	immigrant	custom
communication	artifact	holiday

1. a person who settles in another country _____

2. sharing ideas with others _____

3. a special day _____

4. an object made and used by people _____

5. a building that is important or interesting _____

6. a special way that a group does something _____

 Which word completes each sentence?

1. The wheelbarrow was an _____ of the Chinese.

   a. custom   b. invention

   c. holiday   d. immigrant

2. The Alamo is an example of a _____.

   a. landmark   b. custom

   c. pyramid   d. holiday

Name _____

Color four important American landmarks.

Write why one landmark you colored is important.

_____

_____

Underline the holidays.

Flag Day   February

Labor Day   Martin Luther King, Jr. Day

Saturday   Columbus Day

Write why one holiday you underlined is important.

_____

Circle the picture that shows a calendar from ancient times.

August 2001

Sunday	Monday	Tuesday	Wednesday	Thursday	Friday	Saturday
			1	2	3	4
5	6	7	8	9	10	11
12	13	14	15	16	17	18
19	20	21	22	23	24	25
26	27	28	29	30	31	

© Scott Foresman 2

Unit 6: Skills Test

Reread "An Honest Man" on pages 284–285 of your book.

Draw four things that happened in the story, in order.

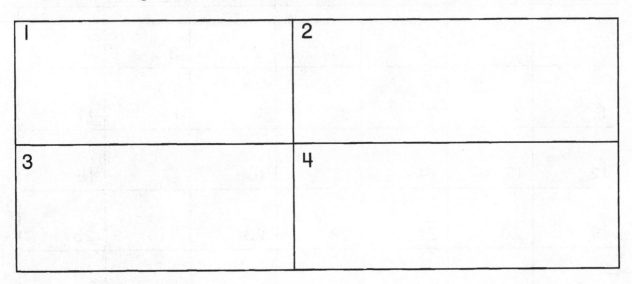

Follow the directions to color the bicycle.

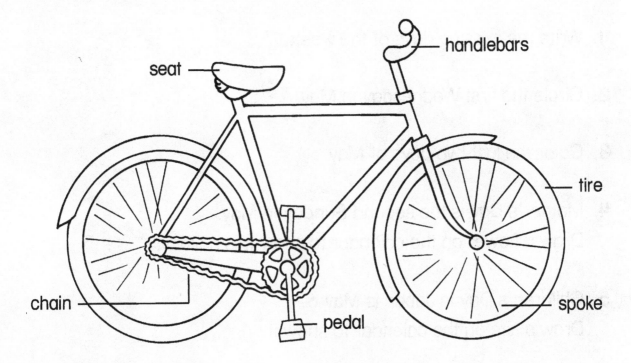

Color the handlebars red.   Color the pedals blue.

Color the tires black.   Color the seat brown.

Follow the directions below.

May 2002

		Tuesday	Wednesday	Thursday		Saturday
			1	2	3	4
5	6	7	8	9	10	11
12	13	14	15	16	17	18
19	20	21	22	23	24	25
26	27	28	29	30	31	

1. Write the missing days of the week.

2. Circle the first Wednesday in May.

3. Color the last two days of May.

4. Mother's Day is the second Sunday in May.
   Draw a flower on the calendar to show this holiday.

5. Children's Day in Japan is May 6.
   Draw a kite on the calendar to show it.

6. Memorial Day is May 27.
   Draw a flag on the calendar to show it.

© Scott Foresman 2

Unit 1: Content Test

Circle a word to finish each sentence.

1. My cousin lives on a very large farm in a ____ area.
   (rural)   urban   community

2. Reading stories about the past is a good way to learn about ____.
   law   (history)   community

3. Who will you ____ for the next time we choose a class president?
   capital   law   (vote)

4. I visited the White House during my trip to the ____ of our country.
   community   suburb   (capital)

TEST PREP Which word completes each sentence?

1. A suburb is a kind of ____.
   a. law   b. history
   c. capital   (d.) community

2. Our town has a ____ against jaywalking.
   a. vote   b. rural
   (c.) law   d. history

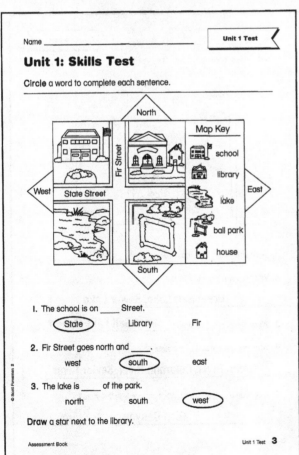

Color the picture that shows a rural community.

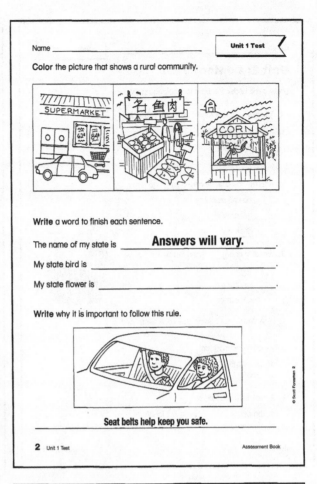

Write a word to finish each sentence.

The name of my state is _____ **Answers will vary.** _____

My state bird is _____.

My state flower is _____.

Write why it is important to follow this rule.

Seat belts help keep you safe.

Unit 1: Skills Test

Circle a word to complete each sentence.

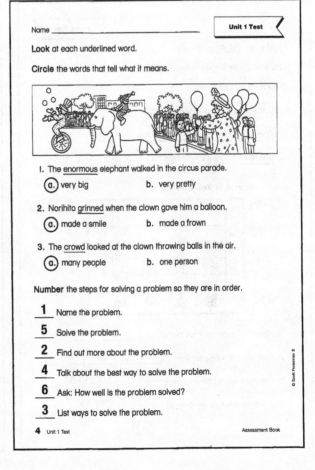

North

Map Key

🏫 school
📚 library
🌊 lake
⚾ ball park
🏠 house

West   State Street   East

South

Fir Street

1. The school is on ____ Street.
   (State)   Library   Fir

2. Fir Street goes north and ____.
   west   (south)   east

3. The lake is ____ of the park.
   north   south   (west)

Draw a star next to the library.

Look at each underlined word.

Circle the words that tell what it means.

1. The enormous elephant walked in the circus parade.
   (a.) very big   b. very pretty

2. Norihito grinned when the clown gave him a balloon.
   (a.) made a smile   b. made a frown

3. The crowd looked at the clown throwing balls in the air.
   (a.) many people   b. one person

Number the steps for solving a problem so they are in order.

1 Name the problem.

5 Solve the problem.

2 Find out more about the problem.

4 Talk about the best way to solve the problem.

6 Ask: How well is the problem solved?

3 List ways to solve the problem.

Unit 2: Content Test

Draw a line under the word that belongs in the sentence.

1. The protection of land, trees, and water is _____.
   <u>conservation</u>
   landform
   geography

2. A family member who lived long ago is my _____.
   natural resource
   geography
   <u>ancestor</u>

3. Wheat is one _____ that a farmer may grow.
   <u>crop</u>
   landform
   consumer

TEST PREP Which word completes each sentence?

1. Air is a very important _____.
   a. geography   (b.) natural resource
   c. crop   d. landform

2. A peninsula is a kind of _____.
   a. producer   (b.) landform
   c. conservation   d. consumer

Think about how natural resources are used.

Write *soil*, *forests*, or *water* under the picture.

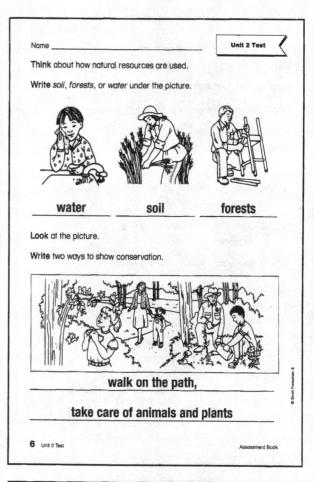

water   soil   forests

Look at the picture.

Write two ways to show conservation.

walk on the path,

take care of animals and plants

Unit 2: Skills Test

Circle the cause in each sentence.

Draw a line under the effect.

(I was hungry) so I ate my sandwich.

(It started to snow) so I put on my boots.

The bird flew away because (the cat jumped up.)

Use the bar graph to answer the questions.

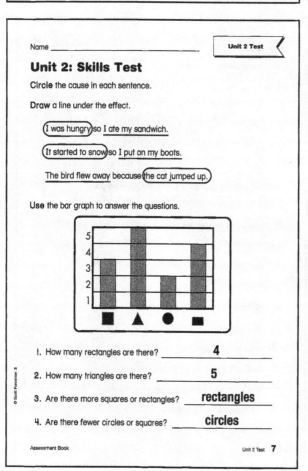

1. How many rectangles are there? _____ **4**

2. How many triangles are there? _____ **5**

3. Are there more squares or rectangles? **rectangles**

4. Are there fewer circles or squares? **circles**

Write answers to the questions about the map.

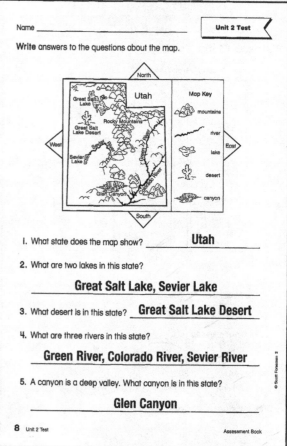

1. What state does the map show? _____ **Utah**

2. What are two lakes in this state?
   Great Salt Lake, Sevier Lake

3. What desert is in this state? **Great Salt Lake Desert**

4. What are three rivers in this state?
   Green River, Colorado River, Sevier River

5. A canyon is a deep valley. What canyon is in this state?
   Glen Canyon

© Scott Foresman 2

26 Answer Key   Assessment Book

Unit 3: Content Test

Write the word that goes with each definition.

trade	services	income	factory

1. the money that someone earns _____ **income** _____

2. a building where people produce goods _____ **factory** _____

3. jobs that people do to help others _____ **services** _____

4. to buy, sell, or exchange goods _____ **trade** _____

TEST PREP Which word completes each sentence?

1. Trains and trucks are a means of _____.
   a. services   b. taxes
   c. goods   (d.) transportation

2. In some places, there is a sales _____ on goods you buy.
   (a.) tax   b. factory
   c. trade   d. barter

Check the things that link countries.

✔ airplane   ___ goods   ✔ ship

✔ truck   ___ factory   ✔ train

Write each word in the correct column.

shoes	rug	food	car	pet	home

Needs	Wants
shoes	pet
food	car
home	rug

Write the names of three service workers.

Answers may include police officer, firefighter, nurse, doctor, teacher, and crossing guard.

Circle two things people can do with their income.

(buy goods)   (save it)   use it to barter

Unit 3: Skills Test

Write to predict what Mario will do.

Mario is having a party in his backyard. The party will start in two hours. Suddenly, the wind starts to blow. Then some thick, black clouds roll in.

Possible answers: Mario will cancel the party; Mario will have the party indoors; Mario will wait to see if the weather changes.

Explain your prediction.

Answers will vary.

Look at these steps for making a decision.

Number the steps in the correct order.

5 Make a decision.

3 List your choices.

2 Gather information.

1 Tell what decision you need to make.

4 Tell what might happen with each choice.

Use the map to complete the sentences.

Write *north*, *south*, *east*, or *west*.

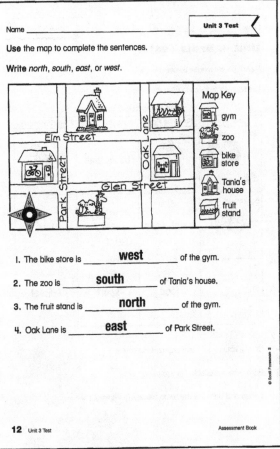

1. The bike store is _____ **west** _____ of the gym.

2. The zoo is _____ **south** _____ of Tania's house.

3. The fruit stand is _____ **north** _____ of the gym.

4. Oak Lane is _____ **east** _____ of Park Street.

Unit 4: Content Test

Circle the word to finish each sentence.

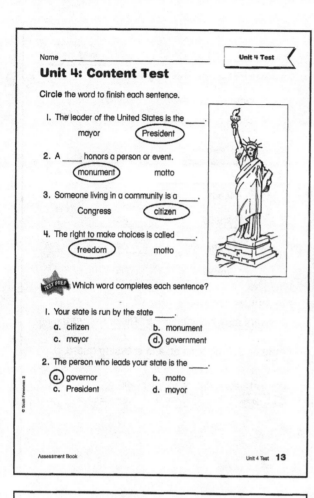

1. The leader of the United States is the ____.
   mayor   (President)

2. A ____ honors a person or event.
   (monument)   motto

3. Someone living in a community is a ____.
   Congress   (citizen)

4. The right to make choices is called ____.
   (freedom)   motto

TEST PREP Which word completes each sentence?

1. Your state is run by the state ____.
   a. citizen   b. monument
   c. mayor   (d.) government

2. The person who leads your state is the ____.
   (a.) governor   b. motto
   c. President   d. mayor

Draw lines to match.

President ●——————● writes and votes on laws.
Congress ●——————● leads the country.
Supreme Court ●——————● says if laws are fair.

Circle the symbols of the United States.

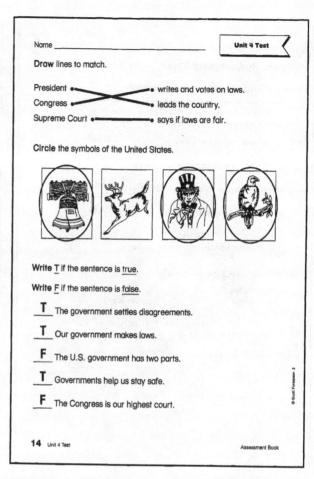

Write T if the sentence is true.

Write F if the sentence is false.

T The government settles disagreements.

T Our government makes laws.

F The U.S. government has two parts.

T Governments help us stay safe.

F The Congress is our highest court.

Unit 4: Skills Test

Read the sentences below.

Draw small pictures to fill in the table.

Our Favorite Things

Classmate	Favorite Food	Favorite Sport	Favorite Animal
Barb		basketball	
Benny	hamburger		bird
Me	food	sport	animal

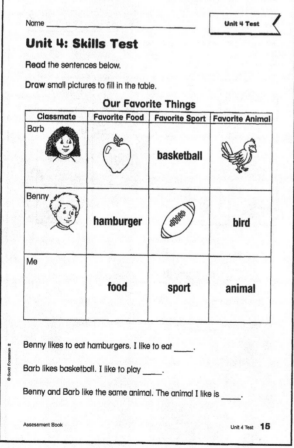

Benny likes to eat hamburgers. I like to eat ____.

Barb likes basketball. I like to play ____.

Benny and Barb like the same animal. The animal I like is ____.

Read about a sunset.

Underline the main idea, and circle the details.

It was a perfect sunset. (The sky was pink and red.) (A cool wind started to blow.) (Light, puffy clouds danced) (against the setting sun.)

Use the map to tell where things are.

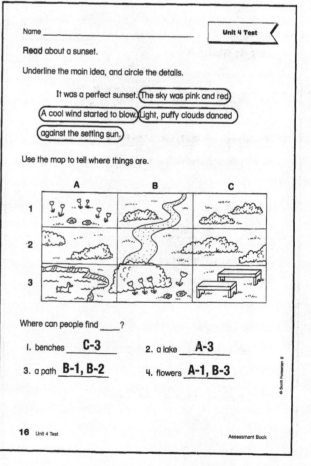

Where can people find ____?

1. benches   **C-3**

2. a lake   **A-3**

3. a path   **B-1, B-2**

4. flowers   **A-1, B-3**

Unit 5: Content Test

Circle a word to finish each sentence.

1. Squanto helped the ____ of Plymouth.
   (colonists)   resources

2. Many colonists wanted their ____ from England.
   shelter   (independence)

3. William Clark was a famous ____.
   (explorer)   colony

4. A place where people live is a ____.
   factory   (shelter)

5. The ____ moved west in covered wagons.
   railroads   (pioneers)

TEST PREP Which word completes each sentence?

1. Eating turkey on Thanksgiving is a ____.
   (a.) tradition   b. shelter
   c. colonist   d. pioneer

2. St. Augustine was a Spanish ____.
   a. shelter   b. tradition
   c. explorer   (d.) colony

© Scott Foresman 2

Assessment Book   Unit 5 Test **17**

Write *X* by each sentence that is true about Native Americans.

X Native Americans used natural resources to build shelters.

X The Sioux wore clothing made from buffalo skins.

X Corn, beans, and squash were grown by the Pueblo.

____ All Native American groups lived on the plains.

X The Powhatan lived along the Atlantic Coast.

Draw lines to match.

Squanto — helped the Jamestown colonists.
Harriet Tubman — helped the Pilgrims survive.
John Smith — helped Lewis and Clark explore.
Sacagawea — led escaping slaves to freedom.

Answer the questions.

What do we celebrate on Independence Day?

   the signing of the Declaration of Independence

Why do Americans celebrate Thanksgiving?

   to give thanks for the things they have

18 Unit 5 Test   Assessment Book

© Scott Foresman 2

Unit 5: Skills Test

Answer the questions about the time line.

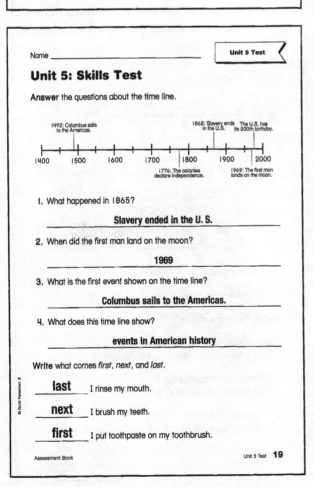

1. What happened in 1865?

   Slavery ended in the U. S.

2. When did the first man land on the moon?

   1969

3. What is the first event shown on the time line?

   Columbus sails to the Americas.

4. What does this time line show?

   events in American history

Write what comes *first*, *next*, and *last*.

last I rinse my mouth.

next I brush my teeth.

first I put toothpaste on my toothbrush.

© Scott Foresman 2

Assessment Book   Unit 5 Test **19**

Use a Map Scale

Look at the map and the map scale.

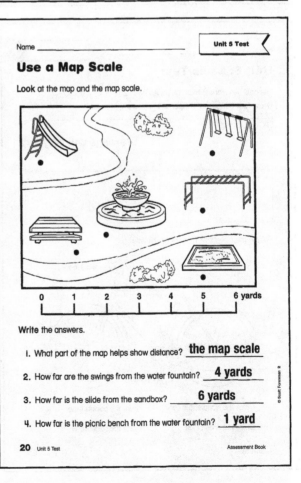

Write the answers.

1. What part of the map helps show distance? **the map scale**

2. How far are the swings from the water fountain? **4 yards**

3. How far is the slide from the sandbox? **6 yards**

4. How far is the picnic bench from the water fountain? **1 yard**

20 Unit 5 Test   Assessment Book

© Scott Foresman 2

© Scott Foresman 2

Unit 6: Content Test

Write the word that goes with each definition.

landmark	immigrant	custom
communication	artifact	holiday

1. a person who settles in another country **immigrant**

2. sharing ideas with others **communication**

3. a special day **holiday**

4. an object made and used by people **artifact**

5. a building that is important or interesting **landmark**

6. a special way that a group does something **custom**

TEST PREP Which word completes each sentence?

1. The wheelbarrow was an _____ of the Chinese.
   a. custom
   (b.) invention
   c. holiday
   d. immigrant

2. The Alamo is an example of a _____.
   (a.) landmark
   b. custom
   c. pyramid
   d. holiday

Color four important American landmarks.

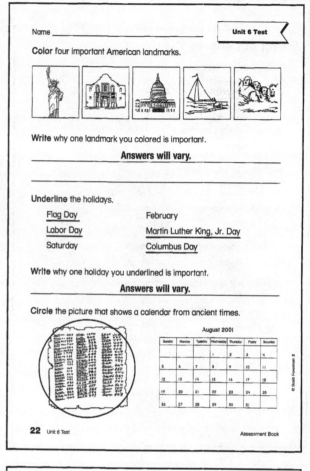

Write why one landmark you colored is important.

Answers will vary.

_____

Underline the holidays.

Flag Day   February

Labor Day   Martin Luther King, Jr. Day

Saturday   Columbus Day

Write why one holiday you underlined is important.

Answers will vary.

Circle the picture that shows a calendar from ancient times.

August 2001

Sunday	Monday	Tuesday	Wednesday	Thursday	Friday	Saturday
			1	2	3	4
5	6	7	8	9	10	11
12	13	14	15	16	17	18
19	20	21	22	23	24	25
26	27	28	29	30	31	

Unit 6: Skills Test

Reread "An Honest Man" on pages 284–285 of your book.
Draw four things that happened in the story, in order.

1	2
	Drawings will vary.
3	4

Follow the directions to color the bicycle.

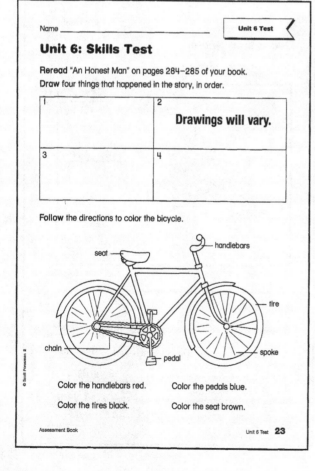

seat — handlebars — tire — chain — pedal — spoke

Color the handlebars red.   Color the pedals blue.

Color the tires black.   Color the seat brown.

Follow the directions below.

May 2002

Sunday	Monday	Tuesday	Wednesday	Thursday	Friday	Saturday
			①	2	3	4
5	6 (kite)	7	8	9	10	11
12 (flower)	13	14	15	16	17	18
19	20	21	22	23	24	25
26	27 (flag)	28	29	30	31	

1. Write the missing days of the week.

2. Circle the first Wednesday in May.

3. Color the last two days of May.

4. Mother's Day is the second Sunday in May.
   Draw a flower on the calendar to show this holiday.

5. Children's Day in Japan is May 6.
   Draw a kite on the calendar to show it.

6. Memorial Day is May 27.
   Draw a flag on the calendar to show it.

NOTES

NOTES

NOTES

NOTES

NOTES

NOTES

NOTES

NOTES

NOTES

NOTES